Native American Library

ONEIDA
History and Culture

Helen Dwyer and Amy M. Stone

Consultant Robert J. Conley
Sequoyah Distinguished Professor at Western Carolina University

Gareth Stevens
Publishing

Please visit our website, www.garethstevens.com. For a free color catalog of all our high-quality books, call toll free 1-800-542-2595 or fax 1-877-542-2596.

Library of Congress Cataloging-in-Publication Data

Dwyer, Helen.
Oneida history and culture / Helen Dwyer and Amy M. Stone.
    p. cm. — (Native American library)
Includes index.
ISBN 978-1-4339-7426-7 (pbk.)
ISBN 978-1-4339-7427-4 (6-pack)
ISBN 978-1-4339-7425-0 (library binding)
1. Oneida Indians—History. 2. Oneida Indians—Social life and customs. I. Stone, Amy M. II. Title.
E99.O45D94 2012
305.897'5543—dc23

                        2011045574

New edition published in 2013 by
Gareth Stevens Publishing
111 East 14th Street, Suite 349
New York, NY 10003

First edition published 2005 by Gareth Stevens Publishing

Copyright © 2013 Gareth Stevens Publishing

Produced by Discovery Books
Project editor: Helen Dwyer
Designer and page production: Sabine Beaupré
Photo researchers: Tom Humphrey and Helen Dwyer
Maps: Stefan Chabluk

Photo credits: AP/Wide World Photos: pp. 31, 32 (both); Corbis: pp. 7 (Marilyn Angel Wynn/Nativestock Pictures), 11, 14 (bottom), 25, 35; Getty Images: pp. 36 (Joe Radle/Newsmakers), 37 (E. Jason Wambsgan/Chicago Tribune), 39 (Sean Gallup); Native Stock: pp. 12, 13, 14 (top), 18, 20, 21, 22, 24, 26, 27; North Wind Picture Archives: p. 15; Oneida Nation Museum of Wisconsin: pp. 17, 19, 23; Oneida Nation of Wisconsin: pp. 10 (bottom), 30, 34; Shutterstock.com: pp. 5 (Alexey Kamenskiy), 28 (Stubblefield Photography); Wikimedia: pp. 8 (U.S. Diplomacy Center), 29 (USDA), 38 (Capt. Hal Pittman/United States Navy).

Printed in the United States of America

CPSIA compliance information: Batch #CS12GS: For further information contact Gareth Stevens, New York, New York at 1-800-542-2595.

CONTENTS

Words that appear in the glossary are printed in **boldface** type the first time they appear in the text.

INTRODUCTION

The Oneidas are a people of New York State, Wisconsin, and Ontario, Canada. They are just one of the many groups of Native Americans who live today in North America. There are well over five hundred Native American tribes in the United States and more than six hundred in Canada. At least three million people in North America consider themselves to be Native Americans. But who are Native Americans, and how do the Oneidas fit into the history of North America's native peoples?

Siberia (Asia) and Alaska (North America) are today separated by an area of ocean named the Bering Strait. During the last ice age, the green area on this map was at times dry land. The Asian ancestors of the Oneidas walked from one continent to the other.

THE FIRST IMMIGRANTS

Native Americans are people whose **ancestors** settled in North America thousands of years ago. These ancestors probably came from eastern parts of Asia. Their **migrations** probably occurred during cold periods called **ice ages**. At these times, sea levels were much lower than they are now. The area between northeastern Asia and Alaska was dry land, so it was possible to walk between the continents.

Scientists are not sure when these migrations took place, but it must have been more than twelve thousand years ago. Around that time, water levels rose and covered the land between Asia and the Americas.

The Cliff Palace at Mesa Verde, Colorado, is the most spectacular example of Native American culture that survives today. It consists of more than 150 rooms and pits built around A.D. 1200 from sandstone blocks.

By around ten thousand years ago, the climate had warmed and was similar to conditions today. The first peoples in North America moved around the continent in small groups, hunting wild animals and collecting a wide variety of plant foods. Gradually these groups spread out and lost contact with each other. They developed separate **cultures** and adopted lifestyles that suited their **environments.**

SETTLING DOWN

Although many tribes continued to gather food and hunt or fish, some Native Americans began to live in settlements and grow crops. Their homes ranged from underground pit houses and huts of mud and thatch to dwellings in cliffs. By 3500 B.C., a plentiful supply of fish in the Pacific Ocean and in rivers had enabled people to settle in large coastal villages from Alaska to Washington State. In the deserts of Arizona more than two thousand years later, farmers constructed hundreds of miles of **irrigation** canals to carry water to their crops.

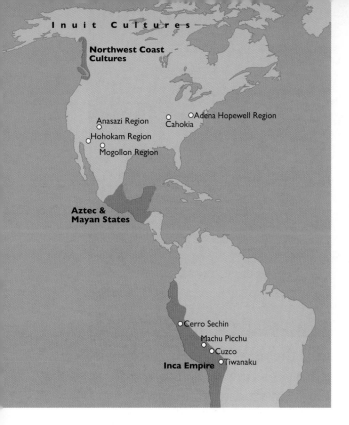

This map highlights some of the main early American cultures.

In the Ohio River valley between 700 B.C. and A.D. 500, people of the Adena and Hopewell cultures built clusters of large burial mounds, such as the Serpent Mound in Ohio, which survives today. In the Mississippi **floodplains**, the native peoples formed complex societies. They created mud and thatch temples on top of flat earth pyramids. Their largest town, Cahokia, in Illinois, contained more than one hundred mounds and may have been home to thirty thousand people.

At some point, the ancestors of the Oneidas arrived in the present-day region of New York State. They lived in villages consisting of longhouses, each of which sheltered several families. They survived by farming, hunting, and fishing. Sometime before A.D. 1500, possibly as early as the twelfth century, the Oneidas joined with four other tribes who spoke similar Iroquoian languages to establish the Haudenosaunee, or Iroquois, **Confederacy**.

CONTACT WITH EUROPEANS

Also around A.D. 1500, European ships reached North America. The first explorers were the Spanish. Armed with guns and riding horses, they took over land and forced the Native Americans to work for them. The Spanish were followed by the British, Dutch, and French, who were looking for land to settle and for opportunities to trade.

A re-created Haudenosaunee village with longhouses made of tree branches and bark.

When Native Americans met these Europeans, they came into contact with diseases, such as smallpox and measles, that they had never experienced before. At least one half of all Native Americans, and possibly many more than that, were unable to overcome these diseases and died. In 1634, measles and smallpox outbreaks killed around two-thirds of the Oneidas.

Guns were also disastrous for Native Americans. At first, only the Europeans had guns, which enabled them to overcome native peoples in fights and battles. Eventually, Native American groups obtained guns and used them in conflicts with each other. Native American groups were also forced to take sides and fight in wars between the French and British. During the American Revolution, the Oneidas sided with the **colonists** against Britain.

Horses, too, had a big influence in Native American lifestyles, especially on the Great Plains. Some groups became horse breeders and traders. People were able to travel greater distances and began to hunt buffalo on horseback. Soon horses became central to Plains trade and social life.

At the end of the 1700s, people of European descent began to migrate over the Appalachian Mountains, looking for new land to farm and exploit. By the middle of the nineteenth century, they had reached the west coast of North America. This expansion was disastrous for Native Americans.

By the mid-1800s, the Oneidas held only 32 acres (13 ha) of land. In the 1820s and 1830s, some Oneidas moved to Wisconsin. Others migrated to Ontario, in Canada, in 1840.

RESERVATION LIFE

Many native peoples were pressured into moving onto **reservations** to the west. The biggest of these reservations later became the U.S. state of Oklahoma. Native Americans who tried to remain in their homelands were attacked and defeated.

GEORGE WASHINGTON
PRESIDENT
1792

In 1792, President George Washington gave this medal to a group of Iroquois at a conference in Philadelphia. It shows an Iroquois and a white American holding peace talks.

New laws in the United States and Canada took away most of the control Native Americans had over their lives. They were expected to give up their cultures and adopt the ways and habits of white Americans. It became a crime to practice their traditional religions. Children were taken from their homes and placed in **boarding schools**, where they were forbidden to speak their native languages.

Despite this **persecution**, many Native Americans clung to their cultures through the first half of the twentieth century. The Society of American Indians was founded in 1911, and its campaign for U.S. citizenship for Native Americans was successful in 1924. Other Native American organizations were formed to promote traditional cultures and to campaign politically for Native American rights.

THE ROAD TO SELF-GOVERNMENT

Despite these campaigns, Native Americans on reservations endured poverty and very low standards of living. Many of them moved away to work and live in cities, where they hoped life would be better. In most cases, they found life just as difficult. They not only faced **discrimination** and **prejudice** but also could not compete successfully for jobs against more established ethnic groups.

In the 1970s, the American Indian Movement (AIM) organized large protests that attracted attention worldwide. They highlighted the problems of unemployment, discrimination, and poverty that Native Americans experienced in North America.

The AIM protests led to changes in policy. Some new laws protected the civil rights of Native Americans, while other laws allowed tribal governments to be formed. Today tribal governments have a wide range of powers. They operate large businesses and run their own schools and health care.

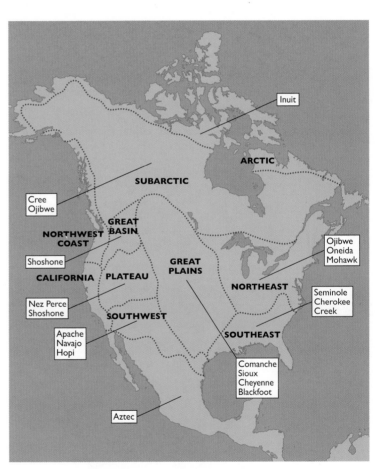

This map of North America highlights the main Native American cultural groups, along with the smaller groups, or tribes, featured in this series of books.

Chapter 1

LAND AND ORIGINS

By the early 1600s, the Oneidas occupied and controlled 6 million acres (2.5 million hectares) of land in what is now central New York State.

LANDS OF THE ONEIDAS

While the Oneidas share a common history, they have followed different paths. About one thousand Oneidas are **enrolled** members of the Oneida Indian **Nation** and live on Oneida homelands near Syracuse, New York. Nearly fifteen thousand Oneidas belong to the Oneida Tribe of Indians of Wisconsin, also called the Oneida Nation of Wisconsin. Tribal members live near Green Bay and Oneida, Wisconsin. The Oneida of the Thames is a rural community of nearly five thousand members in southwestern Ontario, Canada. Three to five thousand Oneidas live on the Six Nations **Reserve** in Ontario, Canada. Other Oneidas live and work throughout the United States and Canada.

Through ritual dances like this one, the Oneidas give thanks for the Creator's many gifts.

In early summer, the Oneidas' strawberry ceremony honors the healing powers of medicinal plants. Strawberries represent the Oneidas' connection to the land.

ONEIDA ORIGINS

Oneidas explain their origins in a traditional story, shared with other Iroquois Indians. Before the earth was made, everyone lived happily in the Sky World. One day, Sky Woman tumbled through a hole in this world, crying for help. As she fell, Sky Woman grabbed some strawberry, tobacco, and corn plants. Some of the creatures that lived in the Water World below heard her cries. A loon caught her and put her on the back of a giant sea turtle. Muskrat carried mud in his paws and placed it on turtle's back. Sky Woman transformed into Mother Earth.

When twin boys were born, the "Good Minded" one created edible plants and harmless animals. The other, known as "Dark Minded," created poisonous plants and dangerous animals. The boys fought with each other to see who was most powerful. Good Minded boy won, but it was not a total victory; it was clear the world would forever be made up of both good and harmful forces.

Chapter 2

HISTORY

MEMBERS OF THE HAUDENOSAUNEE CONFEDERACY

The Mohawk, Onondaga, Cayuga, Seneca, and Oneida Indians lived in what is now New York State and southeastern Canada long before Europeans first encountered them in the early 1600s. As early as the 1400s, Oneida villages spread across nearly 6 million acres (2.5 million hectares) of land in present-day Oneida and Madison Counties in central New York State.

Sacred teachings united the Mohawk, Onondaga, Cayuga, Seneca, and Oneida nations until about the 1100s, when fighting broke out among them. A prophet, the Peacemaker, convinced the nations that warring against each other was foolish. "Because of war," the Peacemaker said, "there is starvation, suffering, and misery. War must cease and everlasting peace must be established

Like other ancient peoples, the Iroquois tied shell beads, or wampum, into patterns that stood for important historical themes. The center object in this wampum belt is the sacred white pine tree, under which the chiefs of the Haudenosaunee (Iroquois) Confederacy met in council. The squares on either side of the tree stand for the five confederacy tribes.

among all peoples." Peacemaker taught people rules to live by called the Great Law of Peace. The five nations then formed a confederacy. Called the League of the Haudenosaunee (or Iroquois Confederacy), the confederacy later influenced the founding fathers of the United States. It served as a government model that respected its members' independence while promoting justice and equal rights for all.

> With endless patience, [Confederacy members] shall carry out their duty. Their firmness shall be tempered with a tenderness for their people. Neither anger nor fury shall find lodging in their minds, and all their words and actions shall be marked by calm deliberation.
>
> *From the Great Law of Peace of the League of the Haudenosaunee, or Iroquois*

Original Names

Made up of the Oneidas, Mohawks, Onondagas, Cayugas, and Senecas, the Iroquois Confederacy members have always called themselves the Haudenosaunee, meaning "People of the Longhouse," which describes their dwellings. They prefer this name to Iroquois, which is a French term based on Irinakhoiw, the Algonquian

Called the Haudenosaunee, or People of the Longhouse, the Iroquois covered their houses with the bark of elm trees. A house sheltered several families belonging to the same **clan**.

Indian word for the Iroquois. The Oneidas' name for themselves is Onyota'a:ka, which means "People of the Standing Stone." According to Oneida tradition, the Standing Stone appears in each new settlement, guiding the Oneidas' search for **fertile** lands, water, and other resources. The English explorers of the 1600s called the Onyota'a:ka the Oneida.

During the 1500s and early 1600s, the Oneidas traded furs for European-made metal items such as knives and farming and building tools.

TROUBLED TIMES

By the early 1500s, European explorers had arrived in North America. In 1634, measles and smallpox, brought to North America by European traders and settlers, spread throughout the nations of the Haudenosaunee Confederacy. Native Americans had no **immunity** to these diseases, which reduced the Oneida population by two-thirds.

Fighting among the Indians also took a toll. The Iroquois nations had traded animal furs for European trade goods, such as iron pots and pans, knives, and axes. Throughout the late 1600s and early 1700s, however, furs became scarce, which led to wars between the Iroquois Nations and their neighbors, the Huron and Algonquian Nations. Many warriors were killed, further reducing the Iroquois and Oneida population.

During the mid-1700s, Oneida chieftain Shikellamy crafted **treaties** with frontier whites that favored the Haudenosaunee, or Iroquois, Confederacy members over the Delaware and Shawnee tribes.

THE AMERICAN REVOLUTION DIVIDES THE CONFEDERACY

British colonists who had settled along the eastern coast of North America wanted their independence from Great Britain and started the American Revolution in 1775. At first, many Haudenosaunee Confederacy leaders thought the Iroquois Nations should remain **neutral.** Finally, however, the Oneidas, under the leadership of Chief Skenandoah, as well as their friends the Tuscaroras, sided with the colonists against the British. The other confederacy nations sided with the British.

The Six Iroquois Nations

After the Tuscarora Indians of present-day North Carolina and South Carolina lost almost all their land to European colonists in the early 1700s, the Oneida and the Cayuga Nations welcomed the Tuscaroras into their villages. They provided land, shelter, and food. In 1715, Tuscarora became the sixth nation in the Iroquois Confederacy.

In this hand-colored print by a European-American artist, British General Burgoyne is shown talking to Native Americans from different tribes, trying to convince them to fight on the side of the British.

Polly Cooper

During one brutally cold winter of the American Revolution, General George Washington's soldiers at Valley Forge, Pennsylvania, nearly starved. Oneida chief Skenandoah and Oneida villagers traveled many miles to take the men bags of corn. One Oneida, Polly Cooper, taught them how to prepare the corn. General George Washington (who later became the first president of the United States) tried to pay her for her help, but she refused. To thank and honor her, General Washington's wife, Martha, bought Polly a shawl and bonnet, which the Oneida people still have.

Many Oneidas fought bravely during the Revolutionary War. During the August 6, 1777, Battle of Oriskany in present-day Oneida County, New York, an Oneida named Honyere Tehawenkarogwen continued firing his gun at the British even after sustaining an injury. While he and nearly five hundred other Oneidas and colonists died in the bloody battle, they were able to stop two British forces from meeting up with each other. This victory helped prevent the British from winning the war.

ONEIDAS LOSE NEARLY ALL THEIR LAND

Following the Revolutionary War, the former colonies grew fast, and settlers were eager to grab the Oneidas' land. The largest loss took place in 1788 when the Oneida Nation signed the Treaty of Fort Schuyler, believing they were **leasing** 5 million acres (2 million ha) of land to New York State. Instead, they were selling it.

The newly formed U.S. government signed the 1794 Treaty of Canandaigua with the Oneidas, assuring them they could keep control of their 6 million acres (2.5 million ha) of land in New York. Despite the federal treaty, New York State made more than thirty fake land treaties with the Oneidas that took their land away. In less than sixty years, from the late 1700s to the mid-1800s, the Oneidas' land base shrank to a mere 32 acres (13 ha).

LEAVING NEW YORK

Between 1821 and 1822, some of the Oneidas paid the Menominee and Winnebago Indians for joint use of 5 million acres (2 million ha) of land along both sides of the Fox River in what is now Wisconsin. In the 1830s, about 650 Oneidas left their homeland for Wisconsin. In 1840, a small group of Oneidas moved to the banks of the Thames River in Ontario, Canada, while another group of about 430 Oneidas moved to Brantford, Ontario, where they bought 5,000 acres (2,000 ha) of land.

Chief Daniel Bread, shown here with his wife, led a group of Oneidas from present-day New York to what is now Wisconsin in 1823.

Mary Cornelius Winder

Even though their New York homeland had shrunk to only 32 acres (13 ha) by the early 1800s, a number of Oneidas refused to move to Wisconsin or Canada. One of their **descendants**, Mary Cornelius Winder, spent much of her life fighting for a return of the Oneidas' New York lands. A mother of eleven children, storekeeper, and **artisan**, she wrote letter after letter to the federal government from the 1920s through the early 1950s, asking it to honor its treaties with the Oneida Nation.

LOSS OF LAND FOR THE WISCONSIN ONEIDAS

In 1827, shortly after the Oneida group had moved to Wisconsin, the Menominees and Winnebagos agreed to a treaty with the federal government that reduced the 5 million acres of land that the Oneidas had paid to live on with them. By 1838, the Oneidas' new lands had shrunk to only 65,000 acres (26,300 ha).

Even that land, however, did not remain within the Wisconsin Oneidas' control for long. The General Allotment Act of 1887 transferred Oneida reservation lands held by the whole tribe into the hands of individuals. By dividing the **communal** land, the U.S. government had hoped to end what remained of Native American tradition, culture, and government. When the government taxed these new individual owners, few understood how and when they should pay their taxes. Many Wisconsin Oneidas missed deadlines and were forced to sell their land to

Meeting in Ontario, Canada, in 1871, the Iroquois Confederacy Council made decisions that benefited all people within the confederacy's six nations. Iroquois leaders are still supposed to base each decision on its effect on peace, the natural world, and the children of the future.

Graduating from high school was a huge **accomplishment** for many teens in the early 1900s. In 1911, however, it also meant these Oneida and other Indian students were forced to give up their traditional culture, clothing, and language.

settle their debts. By 1924, the 65,000-acre Wisconsin Oneida Reservation had shrunk to a few hundred acres.

RECOVERING LAND AND STRENGTH

Further land loss for the Wisconsin Oneidas was halted when Congress passed the Indian Reorganization Act of 1934. This law helped the Wisconsin Oneidas draft a **constitution** and establish a government that was able to buy 1,270 acres (515 ha) of land in 1937 for the Wisconsin Oneidas.

Farming this land, however, did not produce much profit, and the **Great Depression** of the late 1920s and early 1930s put many Wisconsin Oneidas out of the few nonfarming jobs they held. Most people had little money and lived in poor housing. Many suffered from ill health. Despite these problems, the Wisconsin Oneidas slowly regained strength. By the 1970s, the Wisconsin Oneida government had won federal grants that they used to build schools, health clinics, and a youth center.

TRADITIONAL WAY OF LIFE

Chapter 3

A LAND OF PLENTY

The Oneida homeland produced plenty of food for its people. Men hunted the many deer, wild turkeys, rabbits, and other small game that roamed the fields and forests, while women and children planted and harvested gardens that yielded three main crops — corn, beans, and squash. Because the Oneidas considered the environment a part of their family, they called these crops the three sisters. Women and children also gathered berries, nuts, and greens to round out their diet.

The Oneidas practiced slash-and-burn farming; they cleared and burned off an area and then planted. When the soil became less fertile, or able to support crops, they simply moved, leaving one village and starting another.

A Hearty Mealtime

A traditional Oneida meal must have satisfied the hungriest of appetites. As described by a Dutch trader who visited the Oneidas in 1634, a typical meal included corn-based dishes such as cornbread with chestnuts and cornmeal mush, baked and boiled pumpkins, meats, fish, and beans, as well as dried strawberries and blueberries.

Baked cornbread is one of many healthful dishes the Oneidas made from corn.

Oneida longhouses showed that the people valued harmony and balance. The graceful **arc** of bent young trees forms an oval roof, while straight trees provide a contrast.

The streams and rivers emptying into Lake Ontario and the St. Lawrence River held lots of salmon and other fish that the men killed with spears. The men also fished in Oneida Lake as well as the Mohawk, Oswego, and Oneida Rivers.

A HOME FOR ALL

Along streams or lakes where they found fertile land, the Oneidas built their villages of longhouses from elm trees. First, they stripped and dried the bark. Then they drove long, thick branches upright into the ground. These branches formed the sides of the house. The Oneidas bent other branches over the side branches to frame the roof. After tying both sets of branches together with young, flexible trees, they covered the house with the dried bark. Most longhouses stood about 18 feet (5.5 meters) high but could vary in length from 40 to 300 feet (12 to 91 m), depending on the number of families housed within. Doors were placed at both ends of the longhouses.

Each family had its own 20-foot (6-m) section along one side of the longhouse with sleeping bunks and shelves that held clothes, baskets, and household items. Cooking fires lined the center **aisle** of the longhouses every 20 feet (6 m). Families living across the aisle from each other shared a fire. Roof holes above the fire pits let the smoke escape.

CLAN CONNECTIONS

All members of the village belonged to one of three clans — Wolf, Bear, or Turtle. Clan membership depended on the mother. All children born of a Wolf Clan mother belonged to the Wolf Clan. When the Wolf Clan girls grew up, they married someone from outside their clan. Their children, however, remained Wolf Clan members. When boys grew up and married, they, too, had to marry someone outside their clan. The children of these marriages belonged to the mother's clan.

The three eldest women of each of the three clans served as clan leaders. They watched over all the clan's families, helping to settle family disputes and choose marriage partners for young women and men. They also chose the male chiefs, or sachems, who represented their clan in village councils and

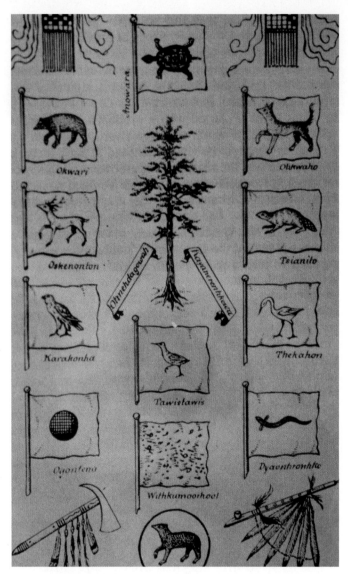

Named after water, land, and sky animals that give special help to people, clans are made up of family groups sharing the same female ancestors. Oneidas belonged to one of three clans — the Bear, the Wolf, and the Turtle — shown on this Iroquois clan chart.

Women, such as Mary Ann Bread shown here, play an important role in Oneida tribal life and are considered equal to men. Bread, daughter of Chief Daniel Bread, earned a degree in nursing and was a member of the Oneida Women's Guild.

in the Iroquois Confederacy. If the clan mothers decided that the chiefs were not fulfilling their responsibilities, they could replace the chiefs with new chiefs.

The Haudenosaunee Confederacy

Respected women leaders from each of the three Oneida clans chose the nine Oneida chiefs who represented the Oneidas in the Haudenosaunee Confederacy. A peacekeeping group, the confederacy's council was made up of fifty sachems — nine Mohawk, nine Oneida, fourteen Onondaga, ten Cayuga, and eight Seneca chiefs. Complex voting and decision-making **procedures** prevented one nation from dominating another.

THE RHYTHM OF LIFE

Villagers devoted much of their time to the important tasks upon which life depended — hunting, gathering, growing, harvesting, and fixing food. Making shelters and clothing took time as well. Until the Oneida people traded fur for European cloth in the 1600s, Oneida women made clothing from deerskins; it took seventeen skins to make enough clothing for a family of five. Both men and women wove cornhusks, grasses, and bark into beautiful and useful storage baskets.

Iroquois Indians made useful and decorative baskets from a variety of grasses and cornhusks. Some versions of the Iroquois creation story say that Sky Woman grabbed a strawberry plant as she fell toward Earth. Perhaps this is why the basket maker wove a strawberry design into her basket.

Time remained, however, for fun and games. Long before the Europeans arrived in North America, the Oneidas played *ga lahs*, a game now known as lacrosse. Hundreds of players would race across mile-long fields, using hickory-wood sticks with rawhide pockets to toss and catch wooden balls.

When the elder men and women told stories, all family members, including the children, listened. Stories kept history alive and made people feel connected.

ONEIDA BELIEFS

The Oneidas believed that a generous Creator had blessed them with many gifts, including Mother Earth and all that she

And the Moral of the Story Is . . .

Some stories, such as one about the fox and the mice, taught lessons. Two mice kept fighting about how to divide a piece of cheese. Each mouse wanted an equal share. When a fox divided it for them, the mice said the pieces were not the same. As the fox kept eating bites from each piece, trying to make them equal, the mice insisted they were not. Finally, the cheese was gone. The fox had eaten it all. The lesson? People who don't learn to share can end up with nothing!

provided. Each and every child was considered a gift from the Creator. The Oneidas never spanked or used physical force to punish their children. With gentle guidance, children learned to respect their elders and to voice their own opinions. The Oneidas believed that the Creator gave every child a special gift. Parents were told to watch for and **nurture** these gifts. If a girl showed a love for music, for example, her parents encouraged her to make instruments or sing and dance.

To express their thanks for the Creator's gifts, the Oneidas held ceremonies throughout the year. Many ceremonies were connected with the change of seasons. After Mother Earth had

Oneida ceremonies honor the land's bounty, both in their traditional lands and in their new home in Wisconsin. In fall, the colorful trees around the Fox River in Wisconsin resemble those of their New York homelands.

The Seven Dancers

According to a traditional tale told by the Oneidas, after seven Iroquois children formed a secret group, their parents used violence to try to break it up. The children sang a sacred and powerful song that lifted them from Earth to the stars. The lonely parents promised the children that if they returned, they would never hit them again. One child tried to return, but he fell and became a shooting star. The other children remained in the heavens, forming a **constellation**. These stars remind Oneida parents to treat their children gently, as the Creator had intended.

During their traditional ceremonies, Iroquois dancers shake colorful rattles made of shells and feathers. Songs and dances celebrate the gifts of life and an ancient **heritage**.

taken a long winter nap, the Oneida people thanked her for awakening with the Midwinter Ceremony, which lasted up to eight days. When the sugar maple sap began to flow in early spring, the Maple Ceremony allowed people to again give thanks — to the blood of the tree for giving **nourishment** to the people. Oneida women made syrup from the sap. During the early spring Seed or Planting Ceremony, the Oneidas expressed their thanks to the Creator for the seeds from which a bounty of crops would grow.

Ceremonies began with prayers of thanks, followed by traditional songs and dances. Rattles, made from turtle shells and gourds, helped the dancers and singers keep tempo. Each man, woman, and child who attended these ceremonies played an equal and valued role, lending voice to a communal chorus of thanks and celebration.

AN EQUAL ROLE FOR ALL

Women and men were considered equal partners. As the givers of life, women exercised responsibility for all things that grew. The men cleared the fields, but the women decided when to plant the seeds and cared for and harvested the crops. Women also tended the young children. Men provided comfort and security by building longhouses, making fires, fighting enemies, and hunting for food. Both women and men taught children the skills they needed for adulthood. While mothers busied themselves with young children, older aunts and grandmothers often taught the older girls how to sew and cook. While young fathers went hunting, older uncles or grandfathers would teach the boys how to detect upcoming weather changes or how to fashion bows and spears from wood — skills needed for hunting and tracking.

Just as they used natural materials to build their homes, the Oneidas used such materials to make toys for the children. This doll is made from deerskin. It shows how traditional Oneidas separated animal fur from skin so both parts could be used.

Oneida Origins

Here are two stories the Oneidas tell about animal species that share their lands. Both stories provide an explanation for animal behavior.

The story of the Hermit Thrush probably evolved because the bird only breeds in forests, which means it is more often heard than seen.

BIRD AND SONGS

Way back in time, only humans could sing. This made the birds unhappy, and the Creator decided that they too should be able to sing. He gathered all the birds together and told them that they must fly up into the sky as high as they were able. Each would then find its own song. The bird that flew the highest would win the most beautiful song.

The little thrush knew he could not fly as high as the larger birds. He decided he would trick the eagle into helping him, so he buried himself secretly in its feathers.

As the Sun rose, all the birds took off. When the Sun set, only the larger birds were left. The following morning, only the eagle was left, but he was very tired. As he gave up and began to fall back to Earth, the thrush took off. He flew up and up until he reached the Land of Happy Spirits. There he heard the most beautiful song in the world. The thrush learned this song, and when he was sure he knew it, he flew back to Earth.

As he approached the ground, he could see all the birds waiting for him, and they were very angry. The thrush was suddenly ashamed because he had cheated. He flew away and hid in the woods. Even today, the Hermit Thrush remains hidden in the trees. Most of the time, he is silent, but when he sings, it is the most beautiful song in the world.

THE MOSQUITO BATTLE

A very long time ago, there were no mosquitoes. Then two giant mosquitoes, the size of trees and with large beaks, appeared next to a river. They would attack any canoes on the river and kill and eat the people in them.

The desperate people eventually fought back. They sent out two giant canoes with all their best warriors, who were armed with bows and arrows as well as clubs and knives. The mosquitoes pierced one of the canoes with their beaks and sank it. The warriors in the other canoe fired countless arrows at the mosquitoes but did little damage. Finally they rowed to the shore and hid behind bushes.

As the mosquitoes followed, the hidden warriors spread out and surrounded them. Now that they were close, the arrows began to have an effect. When all the arrows were used up, the few remaining warriors attacked the weakened mosquitoes with clubs and knives until they had killed them.

Suddenly, millions of tiny mosquitoes appeared out of the blood of the giant mosquitoes and flew away. Since that day, small mosquitoes have taken their revenge on humans by sucking their blood.

Like the giant mosquitoes in this story, modern mosquitoes are found especially in wet places. Eggs are laid in water, and the mosquitoes grow and develop there. They only leave the water as adults.

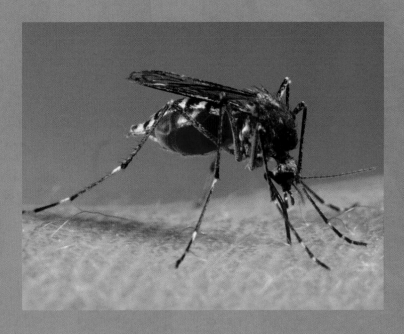

ONEIDAS TODAY

Chapter 4

THE STRONG GROW STRONGER

After years of economic hard times, many residents of Oneida County and the Mohawk Valley of central New York State are prospering. Their good fortune is due, in large part, to efforts of the Oneida Nation. The Oneida-owned Turning Stone **Casino** Resort in Verona, New York, as well as fifteen other Oneida-owned businesses, employ around five thousand people, some of whom are Native Americans. The Turning Stone Resort now includes hotels, restaurants, five golf courses, and a sports center.

Profits from tribal-owned businesses fund more than sixty programs, including housing and health services that support members of the Oneida Nation. A lacrosse and softball field as well as a children and elders center — where elders teach the children Oneida traditions, language, and history — help the Oneidas stay united as a people and keep traditions alive.

The Oneida Nation treasures its children. The nation's vision for the future includes respect for cultural traditions such as ceremony and dance.

The Oneida Nation of Wisconsin's main Oneida Bingo and Casino facility stays open twenty-four hours a day, seven days a week. In 1976, the first Wisconsin Oneida bingo game made $85 in profits. Today, the enterprise earns millions of dollars in profits that help pay for the nation's health, educational, and cultural programs.

WISCONSIN ONEIDAS: A HEALTHY COMMUNITY

Hoping to use its profits to help its people, the Wisconsin Oneidas entered the **gambling** industry in 1976. Profits from bingo games run by a few volunteers paid for a new community recreation center. After the Indian Gaming Regulatory Act of 1988 recognized the right of tribal governments to run and keep the profits from gambling casinos, the Wisconsin Oneidas expanded their efforts into a multimillion dollar enterprise. Gaming profits fund **social services** and schools, create businesses, and allow the nation to buy back Wisconsin Oneida land. The individual tribal members also receive regular payments from the profits.

In 2011, about three thousand people worked for the Oneida Tribe of Wisconsin; nearly half of them were Oneidas. The tribe has repurchased around one-third of their original 65,000 acres (26,300 ha).

To keep the Oneida language alive, Oneida Nations run language classes. The Wisconsin Oneida Nation recognizes Oneida-speaking elders as national treasures. A training program for teachers will ensure that youth understand and speak the language.

EDUCATION

To help its long-range goal of educating future leaders, the Oneida Tribe of Wisconsin opened a tribal school in 1979. The students learn about their Oneida heritage and culture as well as reading, mathematics, science, and social studies. Five of the twenty remaining **fluent** Wisconsin Oneida elders teach the Oneida language to schoolchildren. The tribe provides a number of **scholarships** that help families cover expenses for education beyond high school. Summer job-training programs for teenagers teach job-finding and other useful employment skills.

SOCIAL SERVICES

The Oneida Tribe of Wisconsin also offers extensive health and social services for people who suffer from ill health, drug and alcohol abuse, and other problems. A system of assisted living centers and nursing homes helps take care of Oneida elders.

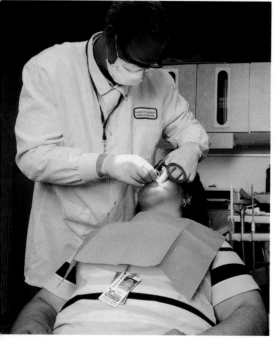

The Wisconsin Oneida Nation has turned casino profits into badly needed health facilities and services for its people. In this reservation-based, modern facility built in 2003, a dentist works on a member's teeth.

WISCONSIN BUSINESSES

Some of the Wisconsin Oneidas' thriving businesses include the Oneida Radisson Hotel in Green Bay, Wisconsin, which houses a gift shop and conference center. In 2003, the Oneidas formed a business partnership called the Four Fires. The Oneidas' partners include the Forest County Potawatomi Community of Wisconsin and two tribes from southern California — the San Manuel Band of Mission Indians and the Viejas Band of Kamewayy Indians. Their first business venture is the construction of a Marriott Residence Inn in Washington, D.C.

TRADITIONS STILL HONORED

With help from the Oneida Tribe's Arts Program, the Wisconsin Oneida still keep the old traditions young. Art program funds allowed Wisconsin Oneida **muralist** Sharon Sarnowski to paint a turtle-shaped lunar calendar in the Norbert Hill Center in Oneida, Wisconsin. Throughout the year, the arts program brings American Indian musicians and writers who perform to enthusiastic audiences in the community. The arts group also sponsors writing workshops as well as fry bread contests and dances, where young and old Oneidas perform native jigging to the sounds of old-time fiddles.

The Oneidas have three nations throughout North America: Oneida of Wisconsin, Oneida of the Thames, and Oneida of New York. While many Oneidas live on national reserves, including the Six Nations Reserve for members of the Iroquois Confederacy, others live throughout the United States and Canada.

Dancers from a Wisconsin Oneida Nation troupe perform at school and civic events throughout northeastern Wisconsin.

Handcrafted from white pine logs, the Oneida Nation's Shako:wi Cultural Center near Syracuse, New York, displays many traditional items such as baskets and rattles. It also serves as a gathering place for Oneidas who wish to learn and practice traditional arts.

ONEIDAS IN CANADA

The Oneida Nation of the Thames is in Ontario, Canada. It has more than five thousand members. These Oneidas bought land in the Thames River region in 1840 after selling their lands in New York. Today they have their own government headed by a chief and a council of ten members.

Indian Community School

A private, intertribal school, the Indian Community School in Milwaukee, Wisconsin, enrolls about 360 children. Ninety of the children are Oneida. In addition to learning traditional subjects such as math and science, students learn core Native American values of bravery, love, truth, wisdom, **humility**, loyalty, and respect. Their education also focuses on Indian spirituality, language, and ceremonies. Teachers believe that they are **counselors** of their children for all time.

Many people attend traditional longhouse ceremonies, and all children are taught the Oneida language in school. The Oneidas of the Thames hold a fair in September with competitions, fireworks, and music. The fair allows Oneida people who have moved away to return and celebrate with old friends.

Just under two thousand Oneidas are members of the Six Nations of the Grand River, near Brantford, Ontario, the largest First Nation in Canada. They share the reservation with the other Iroquois peoples of the Haudenosaunee.

Graham Greene, an Oneida Screen and Television Star

Well-known film and TV actor Graham Greene reads from the Declaration of Independence during a July 4 celebration.

Actor Graham Greene, an Oneida born on the Six Nations Reserve in Ontario, Canada, won fame portraying Kicking Bird, friend to actor Kevin Costner in the 1990 movie *Dances with Wolves*. He has also appeared on many television shows, including *Murder, She Wrote* and *The Red Green Show*. In 2006, he presented *The War That Made America*, a series about the French and Indian War of the mid-1700s.

Showcasing Talents

To increase the presence of Indians on American television screens, Native American actor and producer Sonny Skyhawk started the Oneida Nation's Four Directions talent search. Open to American Indian and First Nation (Canadian Indian) people interested in showcasing their acting, comedy, and writing talents, the search ended in 2003. Bruce King of Santa Fe, New Mexico, and a member of the Oneida Tribe of Wisconsin won for his screenplays *The Woods Will Harbor* and *Evening at the Warbonnet*.

Singer Joanne Shenandoah received a Lifetime Achievement Award from the Native American Music Awards in 2008.

Oneida singer, guitarist, and composer Joanne Shenandoah is the daughter of a Wolf Clan mother of the Oneida Nation. She has produced many albums that have won her three Grammy nominations and a Grammy Award for *Sacred Ground*. She is also an actress, appearing in the movie *The Last Winter* (2007) and in the TV program *First Nations: The Iroquois* (2008). She coauthored a book *Skywoman: Legends of the Iroquois*, which was first published in 1997 and, in 2002, she produced an album called *Skywoman*, in which she was accompanied by the Syracuse Symphony Orchestra.

LITERATURE AND HISTORY

Students at the University of Wisconsin, Madison, can take a class with poet and scholar Roberta Hill, Ph.D., a member of the Oneida Nation of Wisconsin. Hill teaches writing and American Indian Studies classes. She is also writing a **biography** of her grandmother, R. L. Rosa Minoka-Hill, who became a doctor on the Wisconsin Oneida Reservation in the early 1900s.

A STURDY CULTURE

After withstanding tremendous losses over hundreds of years, the Oneida people remain proud of their history, traditions, and ability to thrive. Many Oneidas continue to participate in ceremonies that uphold ancient traditions honoring Mother Earth and all her gifts. By treating Earth and all that springs from her with respect, the Oneidas uphold their responsibility for ensuring the well-being of future generations.

When Oneida elders tell the creation story, Oneida children learn that although the world contains both dark and good forces, the good forces **prevail** — just as the Oneida people have prevailed.

Maria Hinton, born in 1910, is recorded speaking her native Oneida language. Just before her 100th birthday, she finished making 12,000 recordings of Oneida words and stories to help future generations learn the language.

ONEIDA ISSUES

Chapter 5

CASINOS AND TAX

The Oneida Indian Nation does not pay property taxes for its profitable Turning Stone Casino because it is considered Indian land. Since 2005, the local City of Sherrill has claimed that it should be allowed to collect taxes, because the land was bought back by the Oneidas.

U.S. Navy Admiral Edmund Giambastiani speaks with veterans at the Oneida Indian Nation veterans recognition ceremony in Verona, New York, in 2006.

Hiawatha Institute

In 2011, a group of Haudenosaunee leaders, artists, and scholars established the Hiawatha Institute for Indigenous Knowledge. Working together with Syracuse University, they hope to offer degrees in many subjects from a Native American perspective. The courses will be designed by respected native leaders and knowledge keepers and based on traditional teachings. Topics will include Haudenosaunee justice, native art in the Northeast, and Native American contributions to the world.

LAND CLAIMS REJECTED

In the 1970s, the three Oneida tribes joined together to file land claims against the state of New York. After more than thirty years of court hearings, the Oneidas' claims were rejected in 2010. If the Oneidas want to take the matter further, they must appeal to the U.S. Supreme Court.

Animated Stories

Four Directions Productions is a successful Oneida Indian Nation business that specializes in animations of Oneida legends. Its first animated short was called *Raccoon & Crawfish*. It won several awards and was chosen to be screened at the Cannes Film Festival in 2008. In October 2011, Four Directions produced a second animation, *My Home*, which is about being a good neighbor and taking care of the environment.

At the 2008 Cannes Film Festival, the mayor of Cannes receives an Oneida ceremonial gift from Ray Halbritter (left), chief executive officer of the Oneida Indian Nation, and Dale Rodd of Four Directions.

TIMELINE

between 1142 and 1451	The Oneida, Mohawk, Onondaga, Cayuga, and Seneca Nations form the Iroquois League, or Haudenosaunee Confederacy, to put an end to war.
1400s	Oneida villages are spread through 6 million acres (2.5 million hectares) of central New York.
late 1500s –1700s	The Oneidas trade furs and hides for metal pots, metal tools, cloth, and beads brought to North America by the Europeans.
1634	Measles and smallpox epidemics kill thousands of Oneidas and their Iroquois neighbors.
around 1700	Iroquois League at war with their Huron and Algonquian neighbors.
1715	After losing their land to colonists, the Tuscarora Indians from present-day North Carolina and South Carolina move to Oneida country and become the sixth nation in the Iroquois Confederacy.
1766	Missionary Samuel Kirkland urges Oneidas to give up their native customs and replace them with white people's customs.
1775–83	Revolutionary War; many Oneida warriors fight against the British.
1788	By signing the Treaty of Fort Schuyler, the Oneidas are tricked into giving up nearly all their land to New York State.
1820s and 1830s	Many Oneidas move to the Green Bay, Wisconsin, area.
1838	Oneida lands in Wisconsin have shrunk to 65,000 acres (26,300 ha) from an original 5 million acres.

1840	A group of Oneidas moves to the Thames River area in Ontario, Canada. Another group of about 4,300 Oneidas moves to Brantford, Ontario, and buys 5,000 acres (2,000 ha) of land.
1887	General Allotment Act transfers Wisconsin Oneida-held lands into hands of individuals.
1924	Wisconsin Oneida reservation now covers only a few hundred acres.
1934	Indian Reorganization Act helps Wisconsin Oneidas draft a constitution and establish a government.
1937	Wisconsin Oneidas buy 1,270 acres (515 ha) of land.
1970s	Wisconsin Oneidas win federal monies that help them build schools and health clinics.
1976	Wisconsin Oneidas begin a gambling enterprise.
1988	Wisconsin Oneidas start expanding their gambling industry into a multimillion-dollar enterprise.
1993	Oneida Nation of New York opens Turning Stone Casino.
2004	Oneida Nation of Wisconsin employs more people than any other business in northeastern Wisconsin. The Oneida Nation of New York employs nearly four thousand people, restoring economic health to reservation lands.
2005	Oneida Indian Nation in dispute with local City of Sherrill over property taxes.
2010	Oneida land claims rejected.
2011	Hiawatha Institute for Indigenous Knowledge established.

GLOSSARY

accomplishment: something that has been achieved sucessfully.

aisle: a passage between rows of seats or other furniture.

ancestors: people from whom an individual or group is descended.

arc: a curved shape.

artisan: someone skilled in making things by hand.

biography: an account of someone's life, written by someone else.

boarding schools: places where students must live at the school.

casino: a building that has slot machines and other gambling games.

clan: a group of related families.

colonists: settlers in a place.

communal: owned by a group of people rather than by individuals.

confederacy: a group of people, countries, or states united for a common purpose.

constellation: a group of stars that look like they form an image.

constitution: the basic laws and principles of a nation that outline the powers of the government and the rights of the people.

counselors: people trained to give advice and guidance.

culture: the arts, beliefs, and customs that form a people's way of life.

descendants: all the children and children's children of an individual or group; those who come after.

discrimination: unjust treatment usually because of a person's race or sex.

enrolled: registered with a tribe, school, or other organization.

environment: objects and conditions all around that affect living things and communities.

fertile: describes soil that can produce abundant crops.

floodplain: the area of land beside a river or stream that is covered with water during a flood.

fluent: able to easily speak a specific language.

gambling: playing games of chance for money.

Great Depression: the period from 1929 to 1939, when people lost their jobs, homes, farms, and businesses.

heritage: cultural traditions that are passed down from grandparents and parents to children for many years.

humility: a modest view of one's own importance.

ice age: a period of time when the earth is very cold and lots of water in the oceans turns to ice.

immunity: protection from a disease.

irrigation: any system for watering the land to grow plants.

leasing: renting land or rights to someone; the owner keeps ownership of the land but allows someone to use it in exchange for money.

migration: movement from one place to another.

muralist: someone who paints works of art on a wall.

nation: people who have their own customs, laws, and land separate from other nations or peoples.

neutral: not taking sides in an argument.

nourishment: food necessary for health and growth.

nurture: care for and encourage development.

persecution: treating someone or a certain group of people badly over a period of time.

prejudice: dislike or injustice that is not based on reason or experience.

prevail: to triumph or win; to be effective.

procedures: established ways of doing something.

reservation/reserve: land set aside by the U.S. or Canadian government for specific Indian tribes to live on.

sacred: set apart for religious purposes.

scholarships: money for students to attend a school or college.

social services: services provided by the government or other organizations to help the poor, needy, or sick.

treaty: an agreement among two or more nations.

MORE RESOURCES

WEBSITES:

http://www.bigorrin.org/oneida_kids.htm
Online Oneida Indian Fact Sheet for Kids in question-and-answer form with useful links.

http://www.iroquoismuseum.org/
The Learning Longhouse section of the Iroquois Indian Museum website has lots of information about the Haudenosaunee Confederacy as well as the art, music, dance, sports, food, medicine, and beliefs of the peoples of the confederacy.

http://www.joanneshenandoah.com/WELCOME.html
The website of Oneida singer, composer, and actress Joanne Shenandoah.

http://www.native-languages.org/oneida.htm
This website has links to online Oneida language resources.

http://www.oneidaindiannation.com/
New York Oneida Nation news and events as well as cultural and historical information make this an informative site. Take an online tour of the Shako:wi Cultural Center to see beaded handbags, cornhusk dolls, wampum belts, and wood-splint baskets.

http://www.oneidaindiannation.com/culture/legends
Read the story that tells why cornhusk dolls have no face and other traditional tales.

http://www.oneidanation.org/culture/page.aspx?id=5242
The Oneida Tribe of Indians of Wisconsin website contains many interesting pages on the history and culture of the Oneida people.

http://www.rom.on.ca/digs/longhouse
This website has detailed information on Haudenosaunee longhouses.

BOOKS:

Bial, Raymond. *Longhouses (American Community)*. Children's Press, 2005.

Dolbear, Emily J., and Peter Benoit. *The Iroquois (True Books)*. Children's Press, 2011.

Englar, Mary. *The Iroquois: The Six Nations Confederacy (American Indian Nations)*. Capstone Press, 2006.

Gibson, Karen Bush. *Native American History for Kids: With 21 Activities*. Chicago Review Press, 2010.

Graymont, Barbara. *The Iroquois (Indians of North America)*. Chelsea House Publications, 2005.

Johansen, Bruce E. *The Iroquois (The History & Culture of Native Americans)*. Chelsea House Publications, 2010.

Kalman, Bobbie. *Life in a Longhouse Village (Native Nations of North America)*. Crabtree Publishing Company, 2001.

King, David C. *First People*. DK Children, 2008.

Lomberg, Michelle. *The Iroquois (American Indian Art and Culture)*. Chelsea House Publications, 2004.

Lund, Bill. *The Iroquois Indians (Native Peoples)*. Capstone Press, 2006.

Murdoch, David S. *North American Indian (DK Eyewitness Books)*. DK Children, 2005.

Shenandoah, Joanne, and Douglas M. George. *Skywoman: Legends of the Iroquois*. Clear Light Publishers, 2010.

St. Lawrence, Genevieve. *The Iroquois and Their History (We the People)*. Compass Point Books, 2005.

Takacs, Stefanie. *The Iroquois (True Books: American Indians)*. Children's Press, 2004.

Wilcox, Charlotte. *The Iroquois (Native American Histories)*. Lerner Classroom, 2007.

THINGS TO THINK ABOUT AND DO

DEFEND LAND CLAIMS

Pretend you are a lawyer. Write two reasons to give a judge explaining why New York State should return Oneida land to the Oneidas.

PREPARE A TRADITIONAL DISH

Visit the Wisconsin Oneida Nation's website to find a recipe for succotash, a traditional Oneida dish. With adult help, fix the succotash and tell your family why Oneida called corn, beans, and squash the three sisters.

DRAW A PICTURE

Think about how the Oneidas made their longhouses and write down the steps. Then draw a picture of the outside of a longhouse.

WRITING FOR THE SPORTS PAGES

Pretend that you are a sportswriter, and write a short article telling how today's game of lacrosse resembles the game played by traditional Oneidas.

IMAGINE

An Oneida musical group called the Little Big Band blends Native American, country, and rock music. Their songs express good feelings about being a Native American. Think of three feelings an Oneida might have about his or her identity and discuss them in a group.

INDEX